SEPTEMBER 12, 1974

gle: Frank de Kova. Agarn: La
Storch. Parmenter: Ken Berry.
44 HODGEPODGE LODGE
56 FLINTSTONES
5:30 **2 36 44 53 ELECTRIC COMPAN**'
4 FAMILY AFFAIR—Comedy
The twins are captivated by a rode
cowboy—and Bill is fit to be tie
Bill: Brian Keith.
7 CANDLEPINS FOR CASH
9 ROBIN HOOD—Adventure (BW)
Robin (Richard Greene) escorts
Byzantine princess back to he
homeland.
27 GOMER PYLE, USMC
Gomer faces disaster at the Nav
Relief show: the singing Marine ha
lost his voice. Gomer: Jim Nabors.
38 I DREAM OF JEANNIE—Comedy
Jeannie (Barbara Eden) creates
miracle fabric. Groucho Marx plays
himself. Tony: Larry Hagman.
56 GILLIGAN'S ISLAND
A drab visitor to the island becomes
Ginger's glamorous lookalike. Ginger/
Eva: Tina Louise.

EVENING

6:00 **2 36 ZOOM—Children**
3 4 5 6 7 NEWS
8 9 10 12 NEWS
27 PETTICOAT JUNCTION—Comedy
Kate spots trouble: Billie Jo's ex-
beau is dating Betty Jo. Kate: Bea
Benaderet. Betty Jo: Linda Kaye.
38 DICK VAN DYKE—Comedy (BW)
Buddy has a new job—provided he
can break his contract with Alan.
Buddy: Morey Amsterdam. Rob: Dick
Van Dyke. Sally: Rose Marie.

SEPTEMBER 13, 1974

6 NEWS
8 FARMER'S ~~DAUGHTER~~ (BW)
Katy finds a diary written by
Glen's late wife Ann.
27 MOVIE—Science Fiction (BW)
"Missile to the Moon." (1958) Moon
mayhem involving escaped convicts,
rock creatures and a giant spider.
Richard Travis, Cathy Downs. Lido:
K.T. Stevens. (2 hrs.)
38 CAN YOU TOP THIS?—Game
Guests: Ernest Borgnine, Phyllis
Diller and Soupy Sales.
56 MOVIE—Drama (BW)
"Night unto Night." (1949) The turbulent romance of an epileptic scientist and a grieving widow who
meet on Florida's east coast. Ronald Reagan, Viveca Lindfors, Broderick Crawford. Thalia: Rosemary
De Camp. Lisa: Osa Massen. Poole:
Art Baker. Josephine: Lillian Yarbo. Tony: Craig Stevens. Superior
soap opera based on Philip Wylie's novel. (2 hrs.)
12:55 **4 10 NBC NEWS—Edwin Newman**
1:00 **3 MATCH GAME**
4 SOMERSET—Serial
5 6 8 9 ALL MY CHILDREN
—Serial
7 TRUTH OR CONSEQUENCES
10 JACKPOT!—Game
12 WHAT'S MY LINE?
38 JACK LaLANNE
1:30 **3 7 12 AS THE WORLD TURNS**
—Serial
4 10 JEOPARDY!—Game
5 6 8 9 LET'S MAKE A DEAL
—Game
38 FLYING NUN—Comedy
Sr. Bertrille (Sally Field) has a

Friday

6 NEWS

8 FARMER'S DAUGHTER (BW)
Katy finds a diary written by Glen's late wife Ann.

27 MOVIE—Science Fiction (BW)
"Missile to the Moon." (1958) Moon mayhem involving escaped convicts, rock creatures and a giant spider. Richard Travis, Cathy Downs. Lido: K.T. Stevens. (2 hrs.)

38 CAN YOU TOP THIS?—Game
Guests: Ernest Borgnine, Phyllis Diller and Soupy Sales.

56 MOVIE—Drama (BW)
"Night unto Night." (1949) The turbulent romance of an epileptic scientist and a grieving widow who meet on Florida's east coast. Ronald Reagan, Viveca Lindfors, Broderick Crawford. Thalia: Rosemary De Camp. Lisa: Osa Massen. Poole: Art Baker. Josephine: Lillian Yarbo. Tony: Craig Stevens. Superior soap opera based on Philip Wylie's novel. (2 hrs.)

12:55 4 10 NBC NEWS—Edwin Newman

1:00 3 MATCH GAME

4 SOMERSET—Serial

5 6 8 9 ALL MY CHILDREN —Serial

7 TRUTH OR CONSEQUENCES

10 JACKPOT!—Game

12 WHAT'S MY LINE?

38 JACK LaLANNE

1:30 3 7 12 AS THE WORLD TURNS —Serial

4 10 JEOPARDY!—Game

5 6 8 9 LET'S MAKE A DEAL —Game

38 FLYING NUN—Comedy
Sr. Bertrille (Sally Field) has a new admirer: a pelican that thinks she's a bird of a feather. Father Sweeney: Harold Gould. Sr. Jacqueline: Marge Redmond.

2:00 3 7 12 GUIDING LIGHT—Serial

4 10 DAYS OF OUR LIVES—Serial

5 6 8 9 NEWLYWED GAME

38 PORKY PIG AND FRIENDS

2:30 3 7 12 EDGE OF NIGHT—Serial

4 10 DOCTORS—Serial

5 6 8 9 GIRL IN MY LIFE

27 FELIX THE CAT

38 BUGS BUNNY AND FRIENDS

56 TENNESSEE TUXEDO

3:00 2 ELLIOT NORTON REVIEWS

3 7 12 PRICE IS RIGHT—Game

4 10 ANOTHER WORLD—Serial

5 6 8 9 GENERAL HOSPITAL —Serial

27 POPEYE—Cartoon

38 BULLWINKLE

56 UNDERDOG

3:30 2 MAGGIE AND THE BEAUTIFUL MACHINE—Exercise

3 RANGER STATION

4 10 HOW TO SURVIVE A MARRIAGE—Serial

5 6 8 9 ONE LIFE TO LIVE —Serial

7 12 MATCH GAME
Scheduled: Richard Dawson, Brett Somers, Richard Long, Kaye Stevens, Jo Ann Pflug, Charles Nelson Reilly. Host: Gene Rayburn.

27 TIMMY AND LASSIE—Drama (BW)
Lassie picks the winning ticket at a raffle—and the number is held by Ruth (June Lockhart).

38 SUPERMAN—Adventure (BW)
A vengeful crook finds the one element that can destroy Superman —

THE BOOK THAT TAKES YOU BACK

Do You Remember TV?

BY **MICHAEL GITTER, SYLVIE ANAPOL,** AND **ERIKA GLAZER**

**BARNES
& NOBLE
BOOKS**
NEW YORK

DESIGN & ART DIRECTION:
Red Herring Design: Carol Bobolts, Deb Schuler, Adam Chiu, Adria Robbin, Kim Baskinger, and Maureen Rafferty

PHOTO RESEARCH:
Stella Kramer

PHOTOGRAPHY & FOOTAGE:
CBS, Corbis, Greg Davis and Bill Morgan, *Collector's Guide to TV Toys and Memorabilia 1960s and 1970s,*
The Everett Collection, Globe Photos (Jerry Yulsman, Walter Zurlinden), Andrew Goldberg, NBC,
The Motion Picture and Television Photo Archive (Curt Gunther, Marv Newton, Ed Thrasher), Movie Star News,
Jerry Ohlinger's Movie Materials, PhotoDisc, Michael Rubottom, UPI/Corbis-Bettmann

MANY THANKS TO:
We'd like to thank many groups of people who've inspired us, both directly and indirectly, in creating this book:
Our families, with whom in our early lives we watched a lot of television: Michele and Julius Anapol; Paul, Marion and Rudolph
Vaccari; Barbara, Richard, Lory, Kelly, David and Cindy Gitter; Hasya, Alexandra and Zachary Shabtai; Guilford, Diane, Emerson,
Berta and Aaron Glazer. **Our associates at M@x Racks, teachers, friends and great fans of the book** who have given us
constructive criticism, priceless assistance and the occasional bit of grief: Craig Albert, Glenn Albin, John Brancati, Susan
Brustman, Mike Clifford, Howard Courtemanche, Joe Cuervo, Thom Dean, John Dyche, Michele Feeney, Clifford Finn, Shibani
Gambhir, Julia Gillespie, Kara Gilmore, Scott Hankes, Glenn Hinderstein, Peter Levy, Digby Liebovitz, Gene Lisiten, Pam Manela,
Astrid Martheleur, Eric Newill, Mark Pascucci, Mike Reiner, Dana Reston, Steve Robbins, Seth Rosen, Carla Ruben, Giorgio Sestu,
Randi Sharinn, Angela Stevens, Judy Taylor, Joan Thiel, Jim Wayand and Pim Winter. **Our friends at Chronicle**: including our Editor
Sarah Malarkey, Mikyla Bruder, Brenda Tucker, Julia Flagg, Julie Chanter, Tera Killip and Caroline Herter, who greenlighted the first
Do You Remember? —for that we will be forever grateful. We would also like to thank the loyal readers of the original
Do You Remember?, whose response to our efforts prompted another book. And most of all to Carol Bobolts, Deb Schuler,
Stella Kramer and the staff at Red Herring Design, who made this project come to life. Without them, *Do You Remember TV?*
would be little more than a good idea.

This book is dedicated to Jeanine Anapol, Didier Martheleur, Elaine Benson and Erika's uncle, Maurice.
We think they would have enjoyed it.

This edition published in 2005 by Chronicle Books LLC exclusively for Barnes & Noble, Inc.

Copyright © 1999 The Do You Remember? Company, Inc.

The Library of Congress has cataloged the previous edition (ISBN: 0-8118-2305-9). Cataloging-in-Publication data available.

ISBN 0-7607-6157-4

Manufactured in China.

10 9 8 7 6 5 4 3 2 1

It's amazing to think that the first *Do You Remember?* has already sold more than 100,000 copies! After reading the suggestions that poured in, the ones that triggered our fondest memories pertained to television. We immediately began humming favorite theme songs and reliving episodes that made us laugh and cry.

Who doesn't know the words to the *Gilligan's Island* theme song? Many a younger sibling forgot to put the Winky Dinks' protective plastic on the front of the screen, only to find the set completely scribbled on with crayons. A treat while growing up was staying up late to watch *Love American Style*, *Don Kirshner's Rock Concert* or *Bonanza*. And getting up to change the channel, moving around the rabbit ears for better reception or staring mesmerized at early TVs in windows of appliance stores was part of the TV experience for so many of us.

When we thought about all this, we knew that television should be the focus of our next *Do You Remember?* book.

Like the original *Do You Remember?*, the pages here are organized randomly, as memories often are. We must give most of the credit to Carol and the staff at Red Herring Design who once again took a massive list of "stuff" and spun it into a book that is both fun to look at and exciting to pick up again and again. This was no easy task, since a book on television can be a thousand pages without even scratching the surface, but we're sure you won't be disappointed.

As always, we welcome suggestions for the next book. You can E-mail us through our Web site at www.doyouremember.com, or fax us at (212) 873-7223.

Sit back, enjoy *Do You Remember TV?*...and awaaaaaay we go!!!

Michael Sylvie and Erika

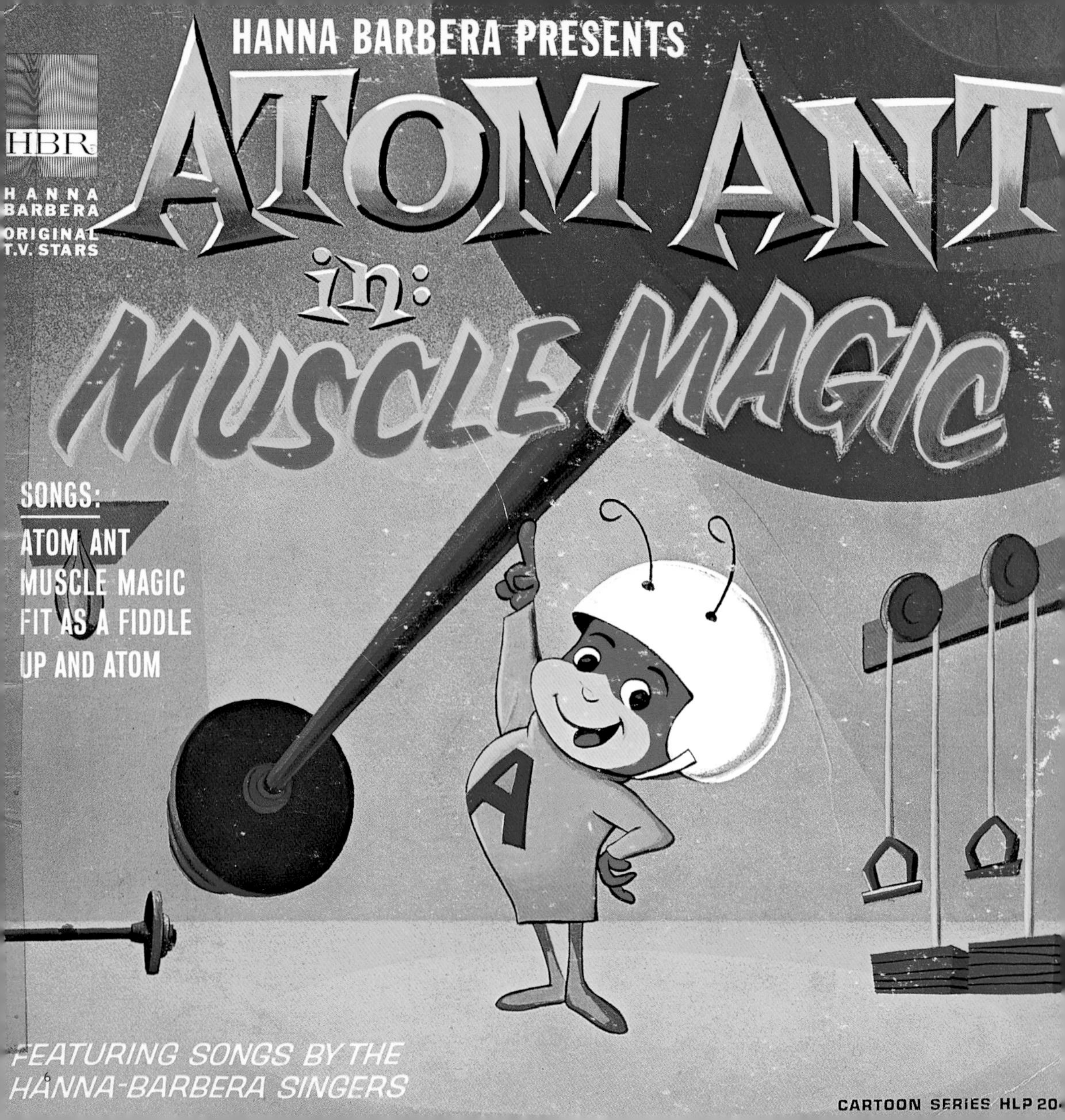

HANNA BARBERA PRESENTS

ATOM ANT
in:
MUSCLE MAGIC

HBR

HANNA
BARBERA
ORIGINAL
T.V. STARS

SONGS:

ATOM ANT
MUSCLE MAGIC
FIT AS A FIDDLE
UP AND ATOM

FEATURING SONGS BY THE
HANNA-BARBERA SINGERS

CARTOON SERIES HLP 20-

Mr. Magoo
Birdman
Fractured Fairytales
Secret Squirrel
Here Comes the Grump
Top Cat
Tennessee Tuxedo
Magilla Gorilla
Underdog
Mighty Mouse
Dastardly & Muttley
Quickdraw McGraw
Ba Ba Looey
Casper, the Friendly Ghost
Huckleberry Hound
Alvin and the Chipmunks
Felix the Cat
Deputy Dawg
Precious Pup
Josie and the Pussycats

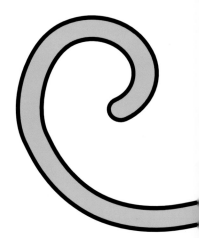

dead ant dead ant dead ant dead ant dead ant dead ant dead ant

Sneezly and Breezly
Chilly Willy
Courageous Cat
Roger Ramjet
The Jetsons
Milton the Monster
Dudley Do-Right
Rocky and Bullwinkle
Looney Tunes

ORANGES
PORANGES
WHO
CARES!?

The Bugaloos

Kimba the White Lion

The Double Deckers

The Hudson Brothers

The Hair Bear Bunch

The Groovie Goolies

The Wacky Races

The Fantastic Four

Yogi Bear and Boo-Boo

The Banana Splits

The Herculoids

Lippy the Lion and Hardy Har Har

Sigmund and the Sea Monsters

Shazzan!

Gumby and Pokey

Hot Wheels

The Krofft Superstar Hour

Isis

Hong Kong Phooey

Speed Racer

Squiddly Diddly

Color 'n Curl

"D" BATTERIES NOT INCLUDED

It's...

A Business
A Great Life
A Hit
A Living
A Man's World
A Problem
A Small World
A Wonderful World
About Time
Academic
Alec Templeton Time
Always Jan
Anybody's Guess
Fun to Know
Garry Shandling's Show
Happening
Magic
News to Me
Not Easy
Polka Time
Punky Brewster
Showtime at the Apollo
Your Bet
Your Business
Your Move

WE LIKE KIX FOR WHAT KIX HAVE GOT, MOMS LIKE KIX FOR WHAT KIX HAVE NOT...

I'M CUCKOO FOR COCOA PUFFS!

SILLY RABBIT, TRIX ARE FOR KIDS!

FOLLOW YOUR NOSE, IT ALWAYS KNOWS...

THEY'RE GRRRRRRRREAT!

HONEYCOMBS BIG, YEAH, YEAH, YEAH, THEY'RE NOT SMALL, NO, NO, NO!

SNAP, CRACKLE, POP!

THEY'RE MAGICALLY DELICIOUS

It's got a good beat and it's easy to dance to, I give it a 10.

Star Search ★ Solid Gold ★ Dance Party U.S.A. ★ The Midnight Special ★ Don Kirshner's Rock Concert

Barry Manilow singing the Bandstand theme

Clearasil and Dippity-Do commercials

"Who wears short shorts?" Nair commercial   Don Cornelius

The Spotlight Dance

Jheri-Curl and Colt 45 commercials

Ob-La-Di, Ob-La-Da

a ------

Love and Marriage

b ------

STAND

c ------

Moon River

d ------

Hᴏᴛ ɪɴ ᴛʜᴇ Cɪᴛʏ

e ------

PAINT IT BLACK

f ------

Reflections

g ------

Georgia on My Mind

h ------

AND SHE WAS

i ------

a *Life Goes On* (sung by Patti LuPone) **b** *Married...with Children* (sung by Frank Sinatra) **c** *Get a Life* (by R.E.M.) **d** *The Andy Williams Show* (by Henry Mancini and Johnny Mercer) **e** *Booker* (sung by Billy Idol) **f** *Tour of Duty* (by The Rolling Stones) **g** *China Beach* (by Diana Ross and The Supremes) **h** *Designing Women* (sung by Ray Charles) **i** *Flying Blind* (by David Byrne, sung by the Talking Heads)

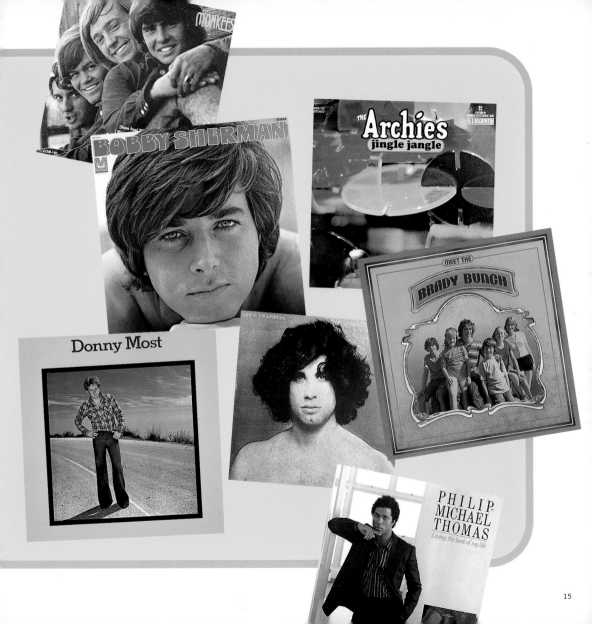

15

flick your Bic

...this tape will self-destruct in five seconds...

17

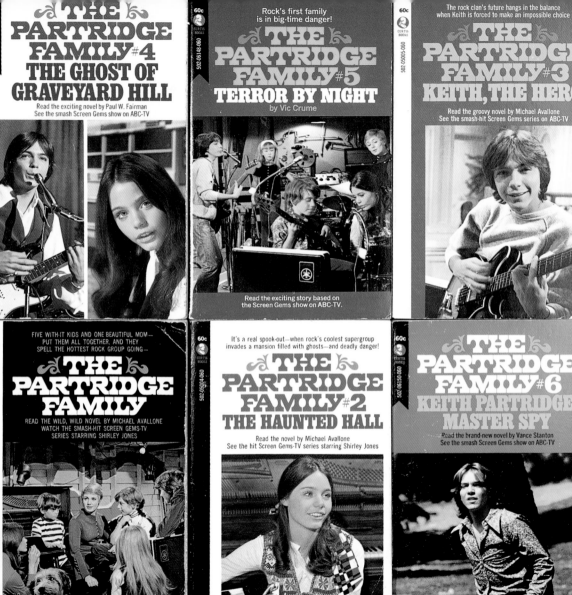

THE PARTRIDGE FAMILY #4
THE GHOST OF GRAVEYARD HILL
Read the exciting novel by Paul W. Fairman
See the smash Screen Gems show on ABC-TV

60¢

Rock's first family is in big-time danger!
THE PARTRIDGE FAMILY #5
TERROR BY NIGHT
by Vic Crume

Read the exciting story based on the Screen Gems show on ABC-TV.

60¢

The rock clan's future hangs in the balance when Keith is forced to make an impossible choice
THE PARTRIDGE FAMILY #3
KEITH, THE HERO
Read the groovy novel by Michael Avallone
See the smash-hit Screen Gems series on ABC-TV

60¢

FIVE WITH-IT KIDS AND ONE BEAUTIFUL MOM— PUT THEM ALL TOGETHER, AND THEY SPELL THE HOTTEST ROCK GROUP GOING—
THE PARTRIDGE FAMILY
READ THE WILD, WILD NOVEL BY MICHAEL AVALLONE
WATCH THE SMASH-HIT SCREEN GEMS-TV SERIES STARRING SHIRLEY JONES

60¢

It's a real spook-out—when rock's coolest supergroup invades a mansion filled with ghosts—and deadly danger!
THE PARTRIDGE FAMILY #2
THE HAUNTED HALL
Read the novel by Michael Avallone
See the hit Screen Gems-TV series starring Shirley Jones

60¢

THE PARTRIDGE FAMILY #6
KEITH PARTRIDGE, MASTER SPY
Read the brand-new novel by Vance Stanton
See the smash Screen Gems show on ABC-TV

MOVIE OF THE WEEK

MOVIE OF THE WEEK

Ode to Billy Joe ★ Death Be Not Proud ★ Dawn: Portrait of a Teenage Runaway ★ Alexander: The Other Side of Dawn ★ Marriage: Year One ★ Brian's Song ★ A Brand New Life ★ The Autobiography of Miss Jane Pittman ★ The Execution of Private Slovik ★ Free to Be...You and Me ★ Sara T.: Portrait of a Teenage Alcoholic ★ The Legend of Lizzie Borden ★ Satan's Triangle ★ Hustling ★ The Boy in the Plastic Bubble ★ Sybil ★ Helter Skelter ★ Raid on Entebbe ★ Little Ladies of the Night ★ The Dark Secret of Harvest Home ★ Please Don't Hit Me, Mom ★ And Your Name Is Jonah ★ Friendly Fire ★ Like Normal People ★ Born Innocent ★ Black Market Baby ★ Scream, Pretty Peggy

AIRWOLF
KNIGHT RIDER
THUNDERBIRDS
THE STREETS OF SAN FRANCISCO
A-TEAM

THE FALL GUY
EQUALIZER
STARSKY & HUTCH
THE FLYING NUN
B.J. AND THE BEAR
FIREBALL XL-5
THE DUKES OF HAZZARD
MIAMI VICE
THE BIONIC WOMAN
SPENCER'S PILOTS
BAA BAA BLACK SHEEP

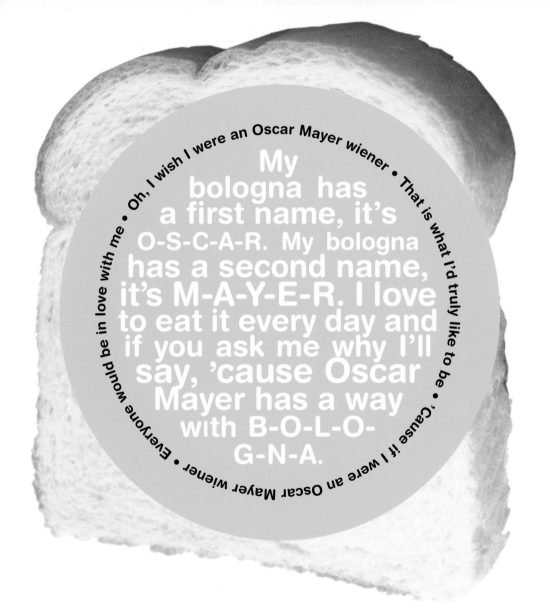

My bologna has a first name, it's O-S-C-A-R. My bologna has a second name, it's M-A-Y-E-R. I love to eat it every day and if you ask me why I'll say, 'cause Oscar Mayer has a way with B-O-L-O-G-N-A.

Oh, I wish I were an Oscar Mayer wiener • That is what I'd truly like to be • 'Cause if I were an Oscar Mayer wiener • Everyone would be in love with me

the red skelton show

the burns and schreiber comedy hour

the carol burnett show

the milton berle show

the soupy sales show

How sweet it is!

Sock it to me!

the jackie gleason show

the sonny and cher show

rowan and martin's laugh-in

mama's family

sid caesar's your show of shows

shields and yarnell

donny and marie

The Devil made me do it!

the captain & tennille

sha-na-na

the smothers brothers comedy hour

the redd foxx comedy hour

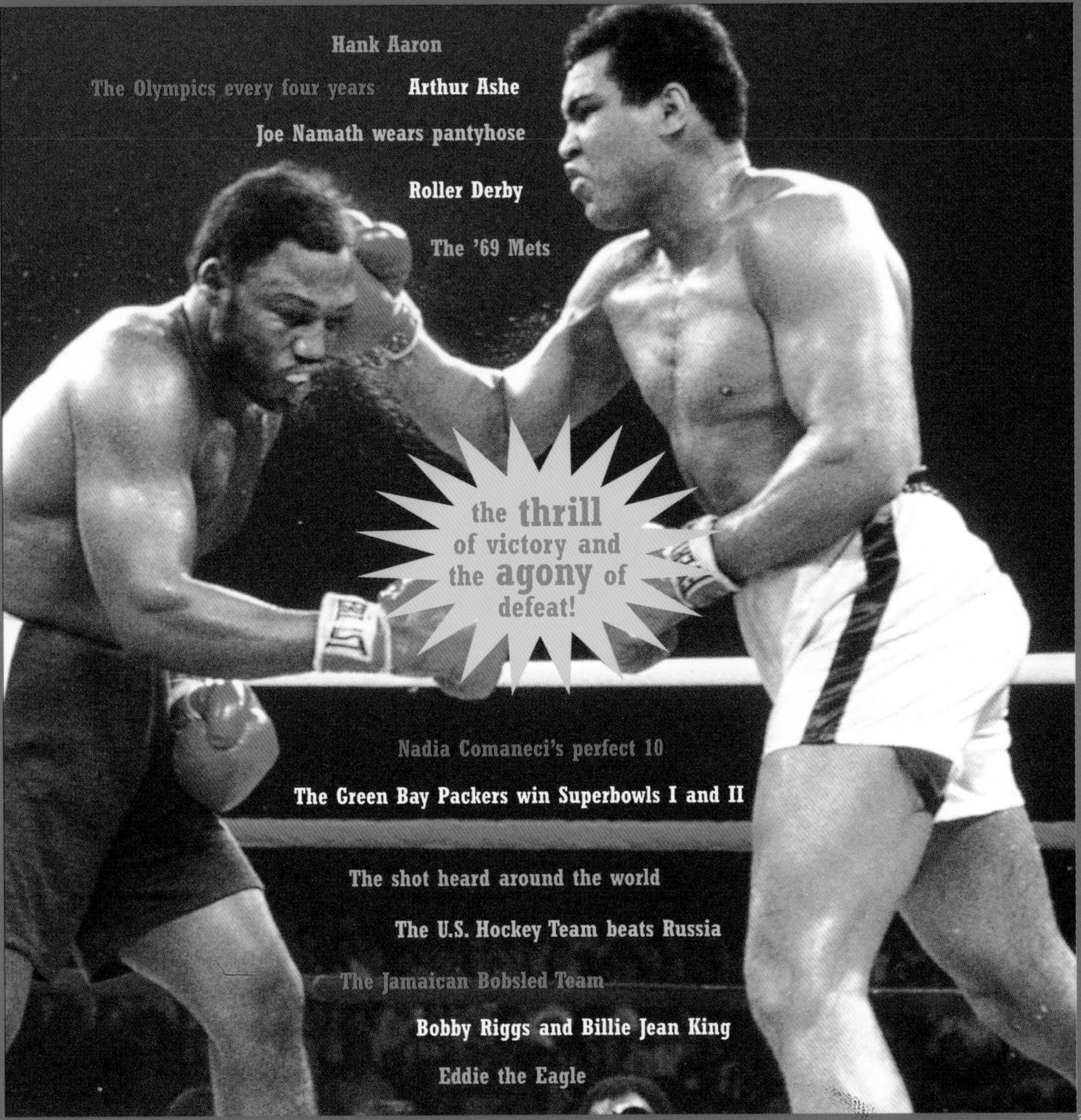

Hank Aaron

The Olympics every four years Arthur Ashe

Joe Namath wears pantyhose

Roller Derby

The '69 Mets

the **thrill** of victory and the **agony** of defeat!

Nadia Comaneci's perfect 10

The Green Bay Packers win Superbowls I and II

The shot heard around the world

The U.S. Hockey Team beats Russia

The Jamaican Bobsled Team

Bobby Riggs and Billie Jean King

Eddie the Eagle

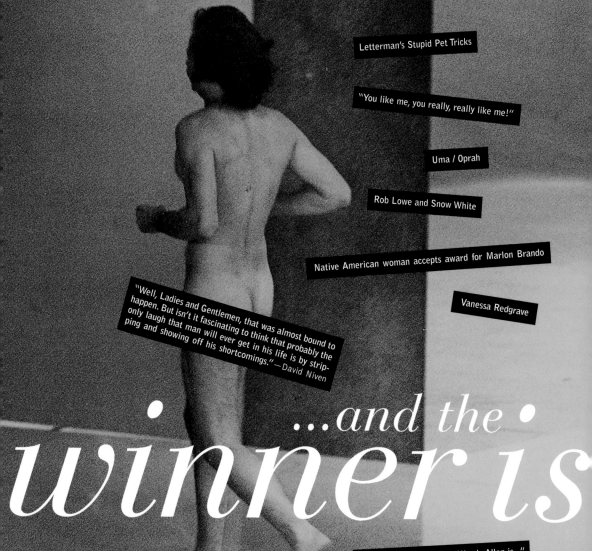

Letterman's Stupid Pet Tricks

"You like me, you really, really like me!"

Uma / Oprah

Rob Lowe and Snow White

Native American woman accepts award for Marlon Brando

Vanessa Redgrave

"Well, Ladies and Gentlemen, that was almost bound to happen. But isn't it fascinating to think that probably the only laugh that man will ever get in his life is by stripping and showing off his shortcomings." —David Niven

...and the

winner is

"Accepting the award for Woody Allen is..."

n't...

Vietnam War **Patty Hearst** Raid on Entebbe **Terrorism at the Munich Olympics** Hostages in Iran **Charles Manson** March on Washington **Love Canal** The Chicago Seven **1960 Democratic and Republican Conventions** "I am not a crook" **Apollo Missions** Martin Luther King Jr. Assassination **The Symbionese Liberation Army** The Gas Crisis **Woodstock** Son of Sam **New York Blackout**

And that's the way it is...

Elapsed Time
01:21.6

TECHNICAL DIFFICULTY

PLEASE
STAND BY

attempt to adjust the picture. We are controlling transmission. If we wish to make it louder, we will bring up the volume. If we wish to make it softer, we will tune it to a whisper. We will control the horizontal. We will control the vertical. We can roll the image; make it flutter. We can change the focus to a soft blur or sharpen it to crystal clarity. For the next hour, sit quietly and we will control all that you see and hear. We repeat: There is nothing wrong with your television set. You are about to participate in a great adventure. You are about to experience the awe and mystery which reaches from the inner mind to the outer limits.

THE OUTER LIMITS

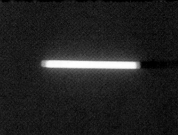

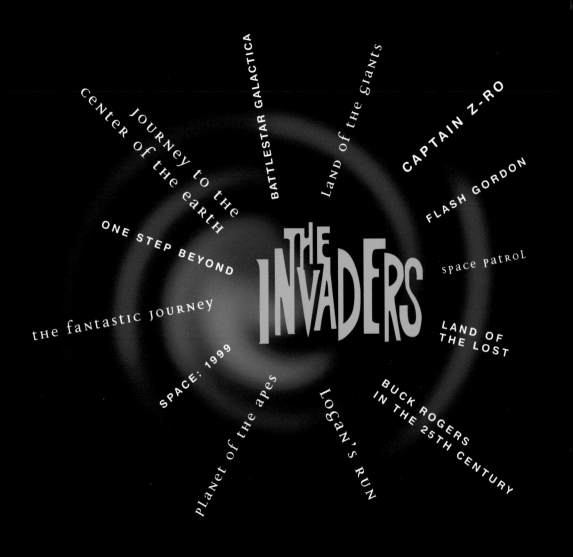

THE INVADERS

BATTLESTAR GALACTICA

LAND OF THE GIANTS

CAPTAIN Z-RO

JOURNEY TO THE center of the earth

FLASH GORDON

ONE STEP BEYOND

space patrol

the fantastic JOURNEY

LAND OF THE LOST

SPACE: 1999

Planet of the apes

BUCK ROGERS IN THE 25TH CENTURY

LOGAN'S RUN

The Love Boat: The Next Wave • Pacific Palisades • Sunset Beach • Malibu Shores • Savannah • 7th Heaven • Kindred: The Embraced • A Season in Purgatory • After Jimmy • Robin's Hoods • Models Inc. • Love on the Run • Burke's Law • University Hospital • Sidney Sheldon's A Stranger in the Mirror • And the Band Played On • The Heights • Melrose Place • Grass Roots • Jailbirds • Beverly Hills, 90210 • The Love Boat: A Valentine Voyage • Rich Men, Single Women • Day One • Nightingales • Cracked Up • International Airport • Glitter • Finder of Lost Loves • Hotel • At Ease • Making of a Male Model • T.J. Hooker • Massarati and the Brain • Dynasty • Strike Force • Hart to Hart • Fantasy Island • Cruise into Terror • The Love Boat • Little Ladies of the Night • Charlie's Angels • Family • One of My Wives Is Missing • Starsky and Hutch • S.W.A.T. • Cry Panic • Death Cruise • Death Sentence • The Girl Who Came Gift-Wrapped • The Bait • The Affair • Snatched • Every Man Needs One • The Bounty Man • The Daughters of Joshua Cabe • The Rookies • The Chill Factor • If Tomorrow Comes • In Broad Daylight • A Taste of Evil • The Last Child • Five Desperate Women • The Reluctant Heroes • The Love War • Crowhaven Farm • The House That Would Not Die • How Awful About Allan • River of Gold • Run, Simon, Run • Yuma • The Ballad of Andy Crockere • The Pigeon • The Monk • Carter's Army • Honey West • Daniel Boone • The Dick Powell Show • Johnny Ringo

PRODUCED BY
Aaron Spelling

I TOLD TWO FRIENDS, AND THEY TOLD TWO FRIENDS, AND SO ON, AND SO ON...

You Bet Your Life / The New Bill Cosby Show / The Electric Company / The Bill Cosby **The Cosby Mysteries** Show / That Was the Week That Was

kodak

Jell-o

old weird harold

I SPY

COS

"You'll never walk alone..."

MY NAME IS CHARLIE THEY WORK FOR ME

A little dab'll do ya! BRYLCREEM Ding-dong, Avon calling

Two, two, two mints in one! CERTS Cleans teeth,

freshens breath, naturally MILK BONE DOG BISCUITS

Thanks! I needed that! MENNEN'S SKIN BRACER Kinda young, AVON

something about an Aqua Velva man AQUA VELVA

Does she...or doesn't she? CLAIROL

FOSTER GRANT Who's that behind those Foster Grants?

kinda now... CHARLIE 99 and 44/100% pure IVORY There's

It takes two hands to handle a Whopper

Twoallbeefpattiesspecialsaucelettucecheesepicklesonionsonasesameseedbun

You deserve a break today, so get up and get away...

Ain't no reason to go anyplace else

McDONALD'S IS YOUR KIND OF PLACE

Where's the

Big Mac, McDLT, a Quarter Pounder with some cheese, Filet-O-Fish, a hamburger, a cheeseburger, a Happy Meal, McNuggets, tasty golden French fries, regular and larger sizes, salad, chef or garden, or a Chicken Salad Oriental, Egg McMuffins, hot hot cakes, and sausage, danish, biscuits too, and for dessert hot apple pie and sundaes, three varieties, a soft serve cone, three kinds of shakes, chocolate chip cookies, and to drink, a Coca-Cola, Diet Coke, Sprite, also an orange juice. I love McDonald's, good time, great taste, and I get this all at one place. The good time, great taste of McDonald's.

Eveningwear...swimwear...

Hold the pickles, hold the lettuce, special orders don't upset us. All we ask is that you let us serve it your way. Have It your way at Burger King.

BOSOM BUDDIES

CHICO AND THE MAN

THROB

MAJOR DAD

WHAT'S HAPPENING

HELLO, LARRY

BENSON

TOO CLOSE FOR COMFORT

OPERATION PETTICOAT

JOE AND VALERIE

THE GOVERNOR AND J.J.

DOUBLE TROUBLE

THE FACTS OF LIFE

BROTHERLY LOVE

BROOKLYN BRIDGE

PICKET FENCES

COACH

BREAKING AWAY

ADAM'S RIB

WE GOT IT MADE

WKRP IN CINCINNATI

SQUARE PEGS

Kiss my grits!

JORDACHE

SASSON

SERGIO VALENTE

Nothing comes between me and my Calvins

CHIC

GLORIA VANDERBILT

NO EXCUSES

Heeeeeeeee

The Mike Douglas Show

The Merv Griffin Show

The Dinah Shore Show

Dinah's Place

The Joan Rivers Show

Tomorrow with Rona Barrett and Tom Snyder

The Dick Cavett Show

David Letterman's morning show

The Steve Allen Show

Geraldo unlocks Capone's vault

Fernwood 2-Night

The Chuck Woolery Show

The Phil Donahue Show

The Arsenio Hall Show

Open End—The David Susskind Show

The Dennis Miller Show

Into the Night starring Rick Dees

The Late Show starring Joan Rivers

The David Frost Show

The Tom Kennedy Show

Charles Perez

ere's

Floyd R. Turbo: American • Ed Ames's
tomahawk throw • Broadcasting from New
York • Skitch Henderson • Jimmy Stewart's
poems • Ed McMahon • Joan Rivers • Tiny
Tim's wedding • Lennon & McCartney •
Doc Severinsen • May 21, 1992 with
Bette Midler and Robin Williams

Wunnerful, wunnerful!

The lovely Anaconnie

The Lennon Sisters

Guy & Ralna

Bobby & Cissy

Myron Floren

Champagne music

Norma Zimmer

61

One of these things is not like the other, one of these things is not the same. Can you guess which thing is not like the others? Now it's time to play our game, time to play our game.

3 FOR THE MONEY

THE THREE STOOGES

WHAT'S BEHIND DOOR NUMBER THREE

BROUGHT TO YOU BY THE NUMBER

WHEN THERE WERE ONLY THREE MAJOR NETWORKS

MY THREE SONS

3-2-1 CONTACT

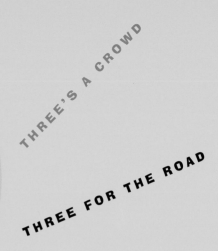

THREE'S A CROWD

THREE FOR THE ROAD

THE THREE MUSKETEERS

THREE ON A MATCH

THREE'S COMPANY

3 GIRLS 3

Come listen to a story 'bout a man named Jed
A poor mountaineer, barely kept his family fed
Then one day he was shootin' at some food
And up through the ground came a-bubblin' crude.
Oil that is. Black gold. Texas tea.
Well, the first thing you know old Jed's a millionaire
The kinfolks said, "Jed, move away from there"
Said, "California is the place you oughta be"
So they loaded up the truck and moved to Beverly.
Hills that is. Swimmin' pools. Movie stars.

The Beverly Hillbillies

Well, now it's time to say goodbye to Jed and all his kin
They would like to thank you for kindly stoppin' in
You're all invited back next week to this locality
To have a heapin' helpin' of their hospitality

Green Acres is the place to be
Farm livin' is the life for me.
Land spreadin' out so far and wide,
Keep Manhattan, just give me that countryside.
New York is where I'd rather stay
I get allergic smelling hay.
I just adore a penthouse view.
Darling, I love you but give me Park Avenue.
The chores!
The stores!
Fresh air!
Times Square!
You are my wife!
Good-bye, city life!
Green Acres we are there.

Come ride the little train that is rollin' down the tracks at the junction,

Petticoat Junction

Forget about your cares, it is time to relax at the junction,
Petticoat Junction
Lotsa curves, you bet, even more when you get to the junction,
Petticoat Junction
There's a little hotel called the Shady Rest, at the junction,
Petticoat Junction
It is run by Kate, come and be her guest at the junction,
Petticoat Junction
And that's uncle Joe.
He's a-movin' kinda slow at the junction,
Petticoat Junction!

Where oh where are you tonight? Why did you leave me here all alone? I searched the world over and I thought I'd found true love, but you met another and PTHHP! you was gone....

65

Billy
↑

↑

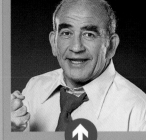

←

↓

The Golden Palace

→

↓

Diagnosis Murder
↑

↑

Spenser: for Hire

→

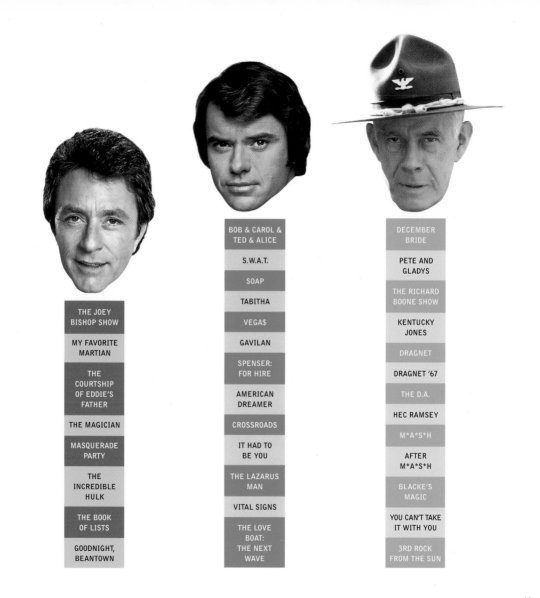

THE JOEY
BISHOP SHOW

MY FAVORITE
MARTIAN

THE
COURTSHIP
OF EDDIE'S
FATHER

THE MAGICIAN

MASQUERADE
PARTY

THE
INCREDIBLE
HULK

THE BOOK
OF LISTS

GOODNIGHT,
BEANTOWN

BOB & CAROL &
TED & ALICE

S.W.A.T.

SOAP

TABITHA

VEGA$

GAVILAN

SPENSER:
FOR HIRE

AMERICAN
DREAMER

CROSSROADS

IT HAD TO
BE YOU

THE LAZARUS
MAN

VITAL SIGNS

THE LOVE
BOAT:
THE NEXT
WAVE

DECEMBER
BRIDE

PETE AND
GLADYS

THE RICHARD
BOONE SHOW

KENTUCKY
JONES

DRAGNET

DRAGNET '67

THE D.A.

HEC RAMSEY

M*A*S*H

AFTER
M*A*S*H

BLACKE'S
MAGIC

YOU CAN'T TAKE
IT WITH YOU

3RD ROCK
FROM THE SUN

This is the city. Los Angeles, California. The story that you are about to see is true. The names have been changed to protect the innocent...

MIAMI
VICE •
BARNABY
JONES •
THE MOD
SQUAD •
MANNIX •   HART TO
THE GIRL   HART • ROUTE 66 •
FROM   HAWAIIAN EYE • THE FALL GUY
U.N.C.L.E.   • THE UNTOUCHABLES
• IT TAKES A   • THE PRISONER • I SPY
THIEF • THE   • CODENAME: FOXFIRE •
ROCKFORD FILES • PETER GUNN • DRAGNET • COLUMBO • MCCLOUD
• BARNEY MILLER • POLICE STORY • VEGA$ • HONEY WEST •
MAGNUM, P.I. • IRONSIDES • KOJAK • MAYBERRY, R.F.D. •
THE STREETS OF SAN FRANCISCO • T.J. HOOKER
• SIMON & SIMON • ADAM-12 • THE AVENGERS • MACMILLAN   THE NEW
& WIFE • FISH • REMINGTON STEELE • MOONLIGHTING • HILL   BREED • NAKED
STREET BLUES • HIGHWAY PATROL • THE HARDY BOYS/NANCY DREW   CITY • THE MOST DEADLY
MYSTERIES • COP ROCK • THE F.B.I. • BANACEK • BARETTA • MIKE   GAME • MOST WANTED
HAMMER •   POLICE WOMAN • CAR 54, WHERE ARE YOU? • CHIPS •   • MATT HELM •
S.W.A.T.   • HAWAII FIVE-O •   STARSKY & HUTCH • 77 SUNSET STRIP •
ELLERY QUEEN   • KATE LOVES A MYSTERY •
CANNON •   PERRY MASON • JAKE
DEVLIN •   & THE FAT-
CRIME   MAN
STORY •
MATLOCK
• THE DETECTIVES •
EYE TO EYE • SECRET AGENT •
RIPTIDE • PETROCELLI • THE OUT-
SIDER • ONE WEST WAIKIKI •
O.S.S.

It's 10 p.m.

Candid Camera
Loretta Young
Hennesey
The Barbara Stanwyck Show
One Step Beyond
The Garry Moore Show
Naked City
Armstrong Circle Theater
The U.S. Steel Hour
Peter Loves Mary
Person to Person
You Bet Your Life
The Detectives
The Twilight Zone
Michael Shayne
The Fight of the Week
Gunsmoke
Adventures in Paradise
The DuPont Show of the Week
Ben Casey
Thriller
Alcoa Premiere
Cain's Hundred
Bob Newhart
The Untouchables
CBS Reports
Sing Along with Mitch
Target: The Corruptors
Voice of Firestone
The New Loretta Young Show
David Brinkley's Journal
The Eleventh Hour
Alfred Hitchcock
The Andy Williams Show

The Rogues
Slattery's People
The Doctors and the Nurses
The Jimmy Dean Show
The Defenders
The Reporter
The Wackiest Ship in the Army
The Steve Lawrence Show
Run for Your Life
CBS Reports
Amos Burke, Secret Agent
I Spy
The Long Hot Summer
The Dean Martin Show
The Man from U.N.C.L.E.
The Big Valley
Jean Arthur
ABC Stage '67
Hawk
Twelve O'Clock High
Laredo
Mission: Impossible
The High Chaparral
The Carol Burnett Show
The Hollywood Palace
Dundee and the Culhane
Good Company
Judd for the Defense
Mannix
The Beautiful Phyllis Diller Show
That's Life
60 Minutes

My Three Sons
The Man and the City
Night Gallery
Owen Marshall: Counselor at Law
The Persuaders
The New Bill Cosby Show
NBC Reports
America
The Julie Andrews Hour
Cannon
Search
Banyon
The Sixth Sense
Medical Center
Police Story
Doc Elliot
Kojak
Love Story
The Streets of San Francisco
NBC Follies
Griff
Barnaby Jones
Get Christie Love!
The Manhunter
Petrocelli
Harry O
Movin' On
The Night Stalker
Police Woman
Nakia
Bronk
Beacon Hill
Joe Forrester

Serpico
Most Wanted
Rafferty
Lou Grant
Baretta
Big Hawaii
The Redd Foxx Comedy Hour
Barnaby Jones
Rosetti and Ryan
Quincy
The Love Boat
Kaz
Lifeline
Vega$
W.E.B.
Flying High
The Eddie Capra Mysteries
Fantasy Island
Dallas
Sword of Justice
Trapper John, M.D.
Prime Time Sunday
The Lazarus Syndrome
The Best of Saturday Night Live
20/20
Kate Loves a Mystery
Eischied
Hart to Hart
Paris
A Man Called Sloane
Flamingo Road
Knots Landing
NBC Magazine

Tucker's Witch
The Quest
Remington Steele
The Devlin Connection
Emerald Point N.A.S.
Bay City Blues
Hotel
Matt Houston
For Love and Honor
The Yellow Rose
Jessie
Miami Vice
Finder of Lost Loves
Cover Up
Hot Pursuit
Our Family Honor
The Equalizer
Spenser: For Hire
Hunter
Jack and Mike
1986
Kay O'Brien
Starman
L.A. Law
Buck James
Thirtysomething
The Law & Harry McGraw
Crime Story
Private Eye
West 57th
Duet
Almost Grown
Midnight Caller
China Beach

Do you know where your children are?

The Jack Paar Program
100 Grand
Breaking Point
East Side, West Side
The Fugitive
The Bell Telephone Hour
Channing
The Danny Kaye Show
Sid Caesar
Here's Edie
The Nurses
Kraft Suspense Theatre

The Jonathan Winters Show
The Outsider
Star Trek
The Bold Ones
Love, American Style
Marcus Welby, M.D.
Hawaii Five-O
Then Came Bronson
It Takes a Thief
Jimmy Durante Presents The Lennon Sisters Hour
Bracken's World

Starsky and Hutch
Kate McShane
Medical Story
Matt Helm
Delvecchio
Executive Suite
Family
Switch
Charlie's Angels
The Blue Knight
The Quest
Van Dyke and Company

Secrets of Midland Hts.
Hill Street Blues
Dynasty
Shannon
Jessica Novak
Strike Force
Falcon Crest
Cassie & Co.
Fitz & Bones
Television: Inside and Out
Cagney & Lacey
St. Elsewhere

Wiseguy
Tattinger's
Heartbeat
Tracey Ullman
Designing Women
Island Son
Quantum Leap
Prime Time Live
Saturday Night with Connie Chung
Mancuso F.B.I.
Comic Strip Live

wonde

kukla, fran and ollie

winky dinks

sesame street

captain kangaroo

the billy barty show

the mickey mouse club

zoom

winchell mahoney and knucklehead

romper room

rama

the electric company

sheriff john

shari lewis and lambchop

howdy doody

75

Howard Borden THE BOB NEWHART SHOW

Stanley & Helen Roper THREE'S COMPANY

Steve & Marcy Rhodes MARRIED...WITH CHILDREN

Fred & Ethel Mertz I LOVE LUCY

Lenny Kowznovski & Andrew "Squiggy" Squigman LAVERNE AND SHIRLEY

George & Louise Jefferson ALL IN THE FAMILY

Tom & Helen Willis THE JEFFERSONS

Milburn & Margaret Drysdale THE BEVERLY HILLBILLIES

Ricky Segall THE PARTRIDGE FAMILY

Barney & Betty Rubble THE FLINTSTONES

Cecily & Gwendolyn Pigeon THE ODD COUPLE

Abner & Gladys Kravitz BEWITCHED

Ron & Ramona Luchesse THE DAYS AND NIGHTS OF MOLLY DODD

Jerry & Millie Helper THE DICK VAN DYKE SHOW

Irwin "Skippy" Handleman FAMILY TIES

Lars & Phyllis Lindstrom THE MARY TYLER MOORE SHOW

Ginny Wrobliki ONE DAY AT A TIME

Ed & Trixie Norton THE HONEYMOONERS

Roger & Kay Addison MR. ED

The Hogans: 555-4656 The Daily Planet: ME 6-0500 The Lawrences: GR 5-5099 The Ricardos: MU 5-9975 The Mertzes: CL 2-0799 The Stephenses: 555-2134

One ringy-dingy...Two ringy-dingys...Three ringy-dingys...Is this the party to whom I am speaking?

The Beaver, 211 Pine Street, Mayfield The Munsters,
1313 Mockingbird Lane Archie and Edith, 704 Hauser Street,
Queens Mr. Kotter, 711 E. Ocean Parkway PLEASE FORWARD 1962 Linden Blvd.
Alice Kramden, 358 Chauncey Street, Brooklyn
Felix Unger & Oscar Madison, 1049 Park Avenue, New York ANN MARIE
344 W. 78TH ST. #4D PLEASE FORWARD 627 E. 54th Street Danny Williams,
505 E. 56th Street, NY The Andersons, 607 S. Maple Street, Springfield
Rhoda Brenda Morganstern PLEASE FORWARD 332 West 46th Street, NYC
Mr. Jethro Bodine, 518 Crestview Drive, Beverly Hills, CA Patty
& Cathy Lane, 8 Remsen Drive, Brooklyn Heights, NY
Dennis Mitchell, 627 Elm Street, Hillsdale Ricky Ricardo 623 E. 68th St. #4a, NY

checking in

the jeffersons maude gloria archie bunker's place **704 hauser**

good times

My name is Rhoda Morganstern. I was born in the Bronx, New York, in December 1941. I've always felt

responsible for World War II. The first thing that I remember liking that liked me back was food. I'm a high

school graduate. I went to art school. I decided to move out of the house when I was twenty-four. My mother

still considers this the day I ran away from home. Eventually, I ran to Minneapolis, where it's cold and I

figured I would keep better, and now I'm back in Manhattan. New York, this is your last chance.

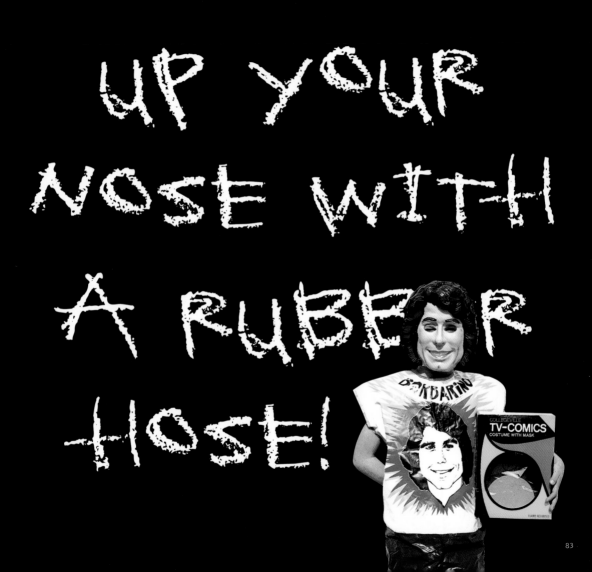

You can learn a lot from a dummy

Like father, like son

ONLY YOU CAN PREVENT FOREST FIRES

Give a hoot! Don't pollute!   TAKE A BITE OUT OF CRIME

A MIND IS A TERRIBLE THING TO WASTE   Kalaka!

Just say no!   This is your brain on drugs

I'd walk a mile for a Camel.

Just what the doctor ordered.

Winston tastes good,
like a cigarette should.

You've come a long way, baby!

I'd rather fight than switch.

More doctors smoke Camels
than any other cigarette!

Tareyton tastes better, charcoal is why.

You can take Salem out of the
country, but you can't take the
country out of Salem.

I'm not a doctor, but I play one on T.V.

The Alternative Factor ✴ The Galileo Seven ✴ Mudd's Women

The Devil In The Dark ✴ Parts I and II ✴ Court Martial ✴ What Are Little Girls Made Of? ✴ The Man Trap ✴ The Enemy Within ✴ Where No Man Has Gone Before

A Taste Of Armageddon ✴ Tomorrow Is Yesterday ✴ Shore Leave ✴ The Menagerie ✴ Charlie X ✴ Balance Of Terror ✴ The Naked Time ✴ The Corbomite Maneuver ✴ The Cage

Errand Of Mercy ✴ Space Seed ✴ This Side Of Paradise ✴ The Squire Of Gothos ✴ Miri ✴ The Conscience Of The King ✴ Dagger Of The Mind

The City On The Edge Of Forever ✴ The Return Of The Archons ✴ Arena

Operation Annihilate

VIDEO KILLED  THE RADIO STAR

Sing Along

On your mark, get set, and go now, got a dream and we just know how, we're gonna make that dream come true—and we'll do it our way, yes, our way...make all our dreams come true for me and you...LAVERNE AND SHIRLEY She's mine alone but luckily for you, if you find a girl to love, only one girl to love, then she'll be that girl, too...THAT GIRL He protects and he saves his friends under the sea, that's where you'll find...DIVER DAN ...still they're cousins, identical cousins, and you'll find they laugh alike, they walk alike, at times they even talk alike; you can lose your mind when cousins are two of a kind...THE PATTY DUKE SHOW Tra-la-la, la-la-la, tra-la-la, la-la-la...THE BANANA SPLITS ADVENTURE HOUR

with Mitch

Phoebe Figalilly is a silly name and so many silly things keep happening; what is this magic thing about Nanny, is it love or is it magic?...NANNY AND THE PROFESSOR ...she's my very own guiding star, a 1928 Porter, that's my mother dear. She helps me through everything I do and I'm so glad she's here...MY MOTHER THE CAR ...we've got a gorilla for sale...full of charm and appeal; handsome, elegant, intelligent, sweet; he's really ideal...THE MAGILLA. GORILLA SHOW ...whatever will be, will be; the future's not ours to see, que séra, séra...THE DORIS DAY SHOW ...wants a gal who's dreamy...wants a gal who's creamy...wants a gal to call his own... DOBIE GILLIS Love is crazy, it's unwise, it can take you by surprise...BRIDGET LOVES BERNIE

DINO

ASTRO

RIN-TIN-TIN

LADADOG

TRAMP

BUCK

BENJI

TIGER

DREYFUS

EDDIE

BANDIT

PETEY

96

dino > the flintstones astro > the jetsons eddie > frasier tramp > my three sons benji > petticoat junction buck > married...with children dreyfus > empty nest bandit > johnny quest petey > the little rascals tiger > the brady bunch ladadog > please, don't eat the daisies

CHUCK WAGON
STEW-LIKE TASTE

Seven Brides for Seven Brothers

20 Mule Team

RAWHIDE

The High Chaparral

Davy Crockett

GUNSMOKE

THE BIG VALLEY

Alias Smith and Jones

Death Valley Days

The Lone Ranger

F-Troop

"DANIEL BOONE WAS A MAN, A BIG MAN..."

THE RIFLEMAN

Branded

HERE COME THE BRIDES

Wagon Train

How The West Was Won

THE WILD WILD WEST

Midnight Caller

Scarecrow and Mrs. King

M Squad

The Man from Interpol

The Ghost and Mrs. Muir

THE SAINT

The Avengers

KNOTS LANDING FALCON CREST HOTEL
PEYTON PLACE DYNASTY THE COLBYS

RICH MAN, POOR MAN MASTER OF THE GAME
BEVERLY HILLS 90210 MODELS INC.

TV GUIDE

WITH SELECTED CABLE / PAY LISTINGS

50¢ Local Programs ◁▷
March 27–April 2, 1982

J.R.'s Revenge
'DALLAS'–MY WAY
By Larry Hagman
Page 2

102

Flipper

Just sit right back and from this tropic port aboard this tiny ship

"You sank my battleship!"

sailing man, the skipper brave and sure. Five passengers

The weather started getting rough,

The Aquanauts

the tiny ship was tossed. If

Sea Hunt

would be lost (the Minnow would be lost). The ship's aground on the

with Gilligan, the Skipper, too, the millionaire

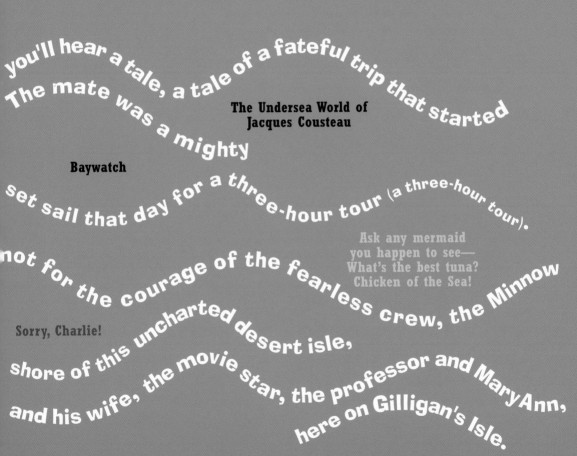

you'll hear a tale, a tale of a fateful trip that started

The Undersea World of
Jacques Cousteau

The mate was a mighty

Baywatch

set sail that day for a three-hour tour (a three-hour tour).

Ask any mermaid
you happen to see—
What's the best tuna?
Chicken of the Sea!

not for the courage of the fearless crew, the Minnow

Sorry, Charlie!

shore of this uncharted desert isle,

and his wife, the movie star, the professor and Mary Ann,

here on Gilligan's Isle.

Don Adams • Edie Adams • Marla Adams • Mason Adams • Charlie Aiken • Edward Albert • Robert Alda • Norman Alden • Kyle Aletter • Debbie Allen • Jayne Meadows Allen • Steve Allen • June Allyson • Don Ameche • Morey Amsterdam • Barbara Anderson • Daryl Anderson • Loni Anderson • Melissa Sue Anderson • Richard Dean Anderson • Richard Anderson • Anthony Andrews • Adam Arkin • Allison Arngrim • Pedro Armendariz Jr. • Bess Armstrong • John Astin • Frankie Avalon • Lois Areno • Desi Arnaz Jr. • Jean Pierre Aumont • Lew Ayres • Catherine Bach • Jim Backus • Vince Baggetta • Kay Ballard • Conrad Bain • Pearl Bailey • Scott Baio • Jack Bannon • Adrienne Barbeau • Cyb Barnstable • Trish Barnstable • Gene Barry • Bill Barty • Dick Bakalyan • Diane Baker • Priscilla Barnes • Doug Barr • Richard Basehart • Kathy Bates • Anne Baxter • Meredith Baxter • Orson Bean • Beene Geoffrey • Ralph Bellamy • Dirk Benedict • Brenda Benet • Lucille Benson • Barbi Benton • Polly Bergen • Lee Bergere • Milton Berle • Warren Berlinger • Jack Bernardi • Ken Berry • Noah Berry Jr. • David Birney • Bill Bixby • Vivian Blaine • Linda Blair • Amanda Blake • Ronee Blakely • Susan Blanchard • Joan Blondell • Lloyd Bochner • Ray Bolger • Frank Bonner • Sonny Bono • Sorrell Booke • Linwood Boomer • Hank Brandt • Bart Braverman • Larry Breeding • Dori Brenner • Lloyd Bridges • Todd Bridges • Melendy Britt • Morgan Brittany • James Broderick • Philip Brown • Woody Brown • Kathie Brown • Ellen Bry • Ray Bucktenika • Bary Burghoff • Paul Burke • Raymond Burr • Dean Butler • Red Buttons • Ruth Buzzi • Edd Byrnes • Sid Caesar • Michael Callan • Charlie Callas • Catherine Campbell • Cab Calloway • Diana Canova • Judy Canova • Diahann Carroll • Victoria Carroll • Jack Carter • Peggy Cass • David Cassidy • Joanna Cassidy • Carol Channing • Cyd Charisse • Chaos • Charo • Sam Chew • William Christopher • Jan Clayton • Debra Clinger • James Coco • Peter Coffield • Dennis Cole • Raymond Cole • Dabney Coleman • Gary Collins • Cissy Colpitts • Gary Coneay • Mike Connors • Hans Conried • Frank Converse • Bert Convy • Jeff Cooper • Alex Cord • Al Corley • Lydia Cornell • Joseph Cotten • Patt Cowley • Bob Crane • Linda Cristal • Cathy Lee Crosby • Mary Crosby • Norm Crosby • Murphy Cross • Scatman Crothers • Patricia Crowley • Pat Crowley • Billy Crystal • Robert Culp • Jane Curtin • Jamie Lee Curtis • Jon Cyphers • Arlene Dahl • Bill Daily • Jimmy Daio • Dallas Cowboy Cheerleaders • Cathryn Damon • Cesare Danoval • Kim Darby • Jennifer Darling • James Darren • Ann B. Davis • Billy Davis Jr. • Clifton Davis • Phyllis Davis • Richard Dawson • Laraine Day • Rosemary DeCamp • Olivia De Havilland • Sandra Dee • Don Defore • Bob Denver • Joyce Dewitt • Dena Dietrich • Phyllis Diller • Donna Dixon • Elinor Donahue • Troy Donahue • Paul Doyle • Denise Dubarry • Ja'Net Dubois • Patrick Duffy • Patty Duke • Sandy Duncan • Nancy Dussault • Patty Dworkin • Leslie Easterbrook • Herb Edelman • Samantha Eggar • Robin Eisenman • Britt Ecklund • Elizabeth the Koala • Ron Ely • Georgia Engel • Erik Estrada • Linda Evans • Maurice Evans • Shelley Fabares • Fabian • Nanette Fabray • Douglas Fairbanks Jr. • Morgan Fairchild • Lola Falana • Antonio Fargas • Jamie Farr • Brian Farrel • Alice Faye • Corey Feldman • Tovah Feldshuh • Norman Fell • Christina Farrare • Conchata Ferrell • Jose Ferrer • Irena Ferris • Fannie Flag • Rhonda Fleming • Charles Frank • Gary Frank • Bonnie Franklin • Pamela Franklin • Char Fontane • Phil Foster • Bernard Fox • Robert Fuller • Annette Funicello • Eva Gabor • Zsa Zsa Gabor • John Gabriel • Betty Garrett • Dick Gautier • John Gavin • Janet Gaynor • Will Geer • Christopher George • Lynda Day George • Maria Gibbs • Melissa Gilbert • Jack Gildord • Richard Gilliland • Lillian Gish • George Gobel • Arthur Godfrey • Arlene Golonka • Ruth Gordon • Grant Goodeve • Lynda Goodfriend • Dody Goodman • Michael Goodwin • Harold Gould • Robert Goulet • Virginia Graham • Fred Grandy • Farley Granger • Karen Grassle • Peter Graves • Lorne Greene • Shecky Greene • James Gregory • Pamela Grier • Rosey Grier • Tammy Grimes • David Groh • Robert Guillaume • Shelley Hack • Joan Hacket • Buddy Hackett • Pat Haden • Jackie Earle Haley • Monty Hall • Tom Hallick • Alan Hale • Brett Halsey • Halston • Nicholas Hammond • Tom Hanks • Ty Hardin • Mark Harmon • Pat Harrington • Jo Anne Harris • Phil Harris • Jenilee Harrison • Lisa Hartman • Peter Haskell • David Hasselhoff • David Hedison • Robert Hegyes • Susan Helfond • Katherine Helmond • Shirley Hemphill • Sherman Hemsley • Florence Henderson • John Hillerman • Kim Holland • Celeste Holm • Telma Hopkins • Susan Howard • Beth Howland • The Hudson Brothers • Gale Hunnicutt • Tab Hunter • Gunilla Hutton • Marty Ingels • Peter Isacksen • Reggie Jackson • Rachel Jacobs • John James • Mark James • Joyce Jameson • Conrad Janis • Maren Jensen • Arte Johnson • Bayn Johnson • Jay Johnson • Van Johnson • Carolyn Jones • Henry Jones • Jack Jones • Elaine Joyce • Ann Julian • Gordon Jump • Shelley Juttner • Steve Kanaly • Caren Kayes • Howard Keel • Stephen Keep • Patsy Kelly • Rozz Kelly • Graham Kennedy • Jayne Kennedy • Ken Kercheval • Joanna Kerns • Brian Kerwin • Meegan King • Werner Klemperer • Richard Kline • Patricia Klous • Ted Knight • Don Knotts • Koock Guich • Bernie Koppell • Nancy Kulp • Laborteaux • Diane Ladd • Judy Landers • David Landsberg • Sue Ane Langdon • Hope Lange • Kim Lankford • Fernando Lamas • Lorenzo Lamas • Dorothy Lamour • Zane Lasky • Margaret Laurence • Marie Laurin • John-Philip Law • Peter Lawford • Carol Lawrence • Tracy Lawrence • Vicki Lawrence • Brianne Leary • Michele Lee • Janet Leigh • Sheila Lenham • Harvey Lembeck • Michael Lembeck • Audra Lindley • Larry Linville • Cleavon Little • Rich Little • Tina Louise • Shelley Long • Dorian Lopinto • Joan Loring • Allen Ludden • Carol Lynley • James MacArthur • Philip Charles Mackenzie • Bob Mackie • Patti MacLeod • Dave Madden • Patty Maloney • Robert Mandan • Irene Mandrell • Stephen Manley • Randolph Mantooth • Rose Marie • Monte Markham • Peter Marshall • Dick Martin • Jared Martin • Pamela Sue Martin • Ross Martin • Nobu McCarthy • Rue McClanahan • Marilyn McCoo • Kent McCord • Patty McCormack • Maureen McCormick • Pat McCormick • Mary McDonough • Roddy McDowall • Darren McGaven • Nancy McKeon • John McInerie • Allyn An McLerie • Kristy McNichol • Audrey Meadows • Anne Meara • John Meehan • Eddie Mekka • Gabriel Melgar • Heather Menzies • Lee Meriwether • Ethel Merman • Dina Merrill • Vera Miles • Ray Milland • Ann Miller • Denise Miller • Donna Mills • Hayley Mills • Juliet Mills • Sir John Mills • Keith Mitchell • Mary Ann Mobley • Al Molinaro • Kelly Monteith • Belinda J. Montgomery • Lynne Moody • Melba Moore • Terry Moore • Erin Moran • Cindy Morgan • Debbi Morgan • Dennis Morgan • Harry Morgan • Henry Morgan • Jaye P. Morgan • Pat Morita • Greg Morris • Karen Morrow • Donny Most • Diana Muldaur • Richard Mulligan • Robert Mulligan • Ben Murphy • Jim Nabors • Joe Namath • Mildred Natwick • Melinda Naud • Connie Needham • Barry Nelson • David Nelson • Harriet Nelson • Rick Nelson • Lois Nettleton • Julie Newmar • Denise Nicholas • Denise Nicholas-Hill • Leslie Nielson • James Noble • Trisha Noble • Jeannette Nolan • Kathleen Nolan • Christopher Norris • Judy Norton-Taylor • Shelly Novack • Louis Nye • Hugh O'Brian • Donald O'Connor • Lani O'Grady • Randi Oakes • Susan Oliver • Donny Osmond • Jimmy Osmond • Lawanda Page • Janis Paige • Ron Palillio • Betsy Palmer • Eleanor Parker • Bert Parks • Catherine Parks • Minnie Pearl • Meeno Peluce • Donna Pescow • Joanna Petter • Jo Ann Pflug • Mackenzie Phillips • Michelle Phillips • Mark Pinter • Eve Plumb • The Pointer Sisters • Don Porter • Markie Post • Tom Poston • Jane Powell • Randall Powell • Joan Prather • Vincent Price • Juliet Prowse • Charlotte Rae • Dacko Rambo • Gene Rayburn • Martha Raye • Robert Rayes • Helen Reddy • Robert Reed • Tracy Reed • Della Reese • Charles Nelson Reilly • Alejandro Rey • Debbie Reynolds • Barbara Rhoades • Adam Rich • Susan Richardson • John Ritter • Doris Roberts • Pernell Roberts • Tanya Roberts • Tony Roberts • Dale Robertson • John Mark Robinson • Ginger Rogers • Marion Ross • Dan Rowan • Misty Rowe • Richard Roundtree • John Rubinstein • Barbara Rush • Nipsey Russell • Soupy Sales • Jennifer Salt • Isabel Sanford • Dean Santoro • Dick Sargent • Brad Savage • Ronnie Scribner • Natalie Schafer • Ronnie Schell • Avery Schreiber • Debralee Scott • Martha Scott • Mark Serra • Jennifer Shaw • Dick Shawn • Mark Shera • Bobby Sherman • Bobby Short • Stephen Shortridge • Sonny Shrover • Sylvia Sidney • Charles Siebeert • Phil Silvers • Walker Slezak • Jaclyn Smith • Rex Smith • Shelley Smith • Tom Smothers • Jack Somack • Brett Somers • Suzanne Somers • Elke Sommer • Laurette Spang • Camilla Spary • Jill St. John • Robert Stack • Jim Stafford • Bernadette Stanis • Jim Stafford • Laraine Stephens • Skip Stephenson • Connie Stevens • Craig Stevens • Marti Stevens • Mclean Stevenson • Trish Stewart • Jerry Stiller • Larry Storch • Susan Strasper • WK Stratton • Barry Sullivan • Shauna Sullivan • Susan Sullivan • Loretta Swit • Brenda Sykes • Robert Symonds • Jeff Tambor • Vic Tayback • Leigh Taylor-Young • Toni Tennille • Lauren Tewes • Mark Thomas • Kevin Tighe • Charlene Tilton • Johnny Timko • Michele Tobin • Berlinda Tolbert • Fred Travelena • Ellen Travolta • Michael Tucci • Forrest Tucker • Tanya Tucker • Leslie Uggams • Bob Urich • Robert Urich • Karen Valentine • Bobby Van • Joan Van Ark • Barry Van Dyke • Dick Van Patten • Vincent Van Patton • Gloria Vanderbilt • Robert Vau • Ben Vereen • Abe Vigoda • The Village People • Sal Viscuso • Lyle Waggoner • Marcia Wallace • Jimmie Walker • Nancy Walker • Jessica Walter • Carlene Watkins • Vernee Watson • Kristina Wayborn • Patrick Wayne • Dawn Wells • Judy West • Jill Whelan • Andjesse White • Betty White • Larry Wilcox • Fred Willard • Anson Williams • Paul Williams • Desmond Wilson • Flip Wilson • William Windom • Edward Winter • Jane Withers • Alex Woddard • Jo Anne Worley • Jane Wyatt • Jane Wyman • Dana Wynter • Alan Young • Michael Young • Jonny Yune • Michael Zaslow • Stephanie Zimbalist

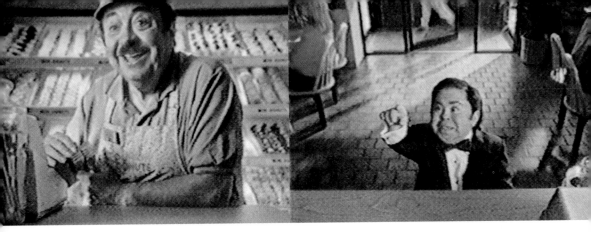

THE PLAIN, THE PLAIN!
NO, THE GLAZED, THE GLAZED!

bridget loves bernie

trixie

gloria

ethel

alice

pam

olivia

blanche

betty

joanie loves chachi

julie

winnie

laura

pickles

georgette

diane

caroline

buddy loves pickles (the dick van dyke show) • doug loves julie (days of our lives) • ted loves georgette (the mary tyler moore show) • felix loved gloria (the odd couple) • bobby loves pam (dallas) • kevin loves winnie (the wonder years) • sam loves diane (cheers) • fred loves ethel (I love lucy) • john loves olivia (the waltons) • charles loves caroline (little house on the prairie) • luke loves laura (general hospital) • oscar loved blanche (the odd couple) • barney loves betty (the flintstones) • sam loves alice (the brady bunch) • ed loves trixie (the honeymooners) 109

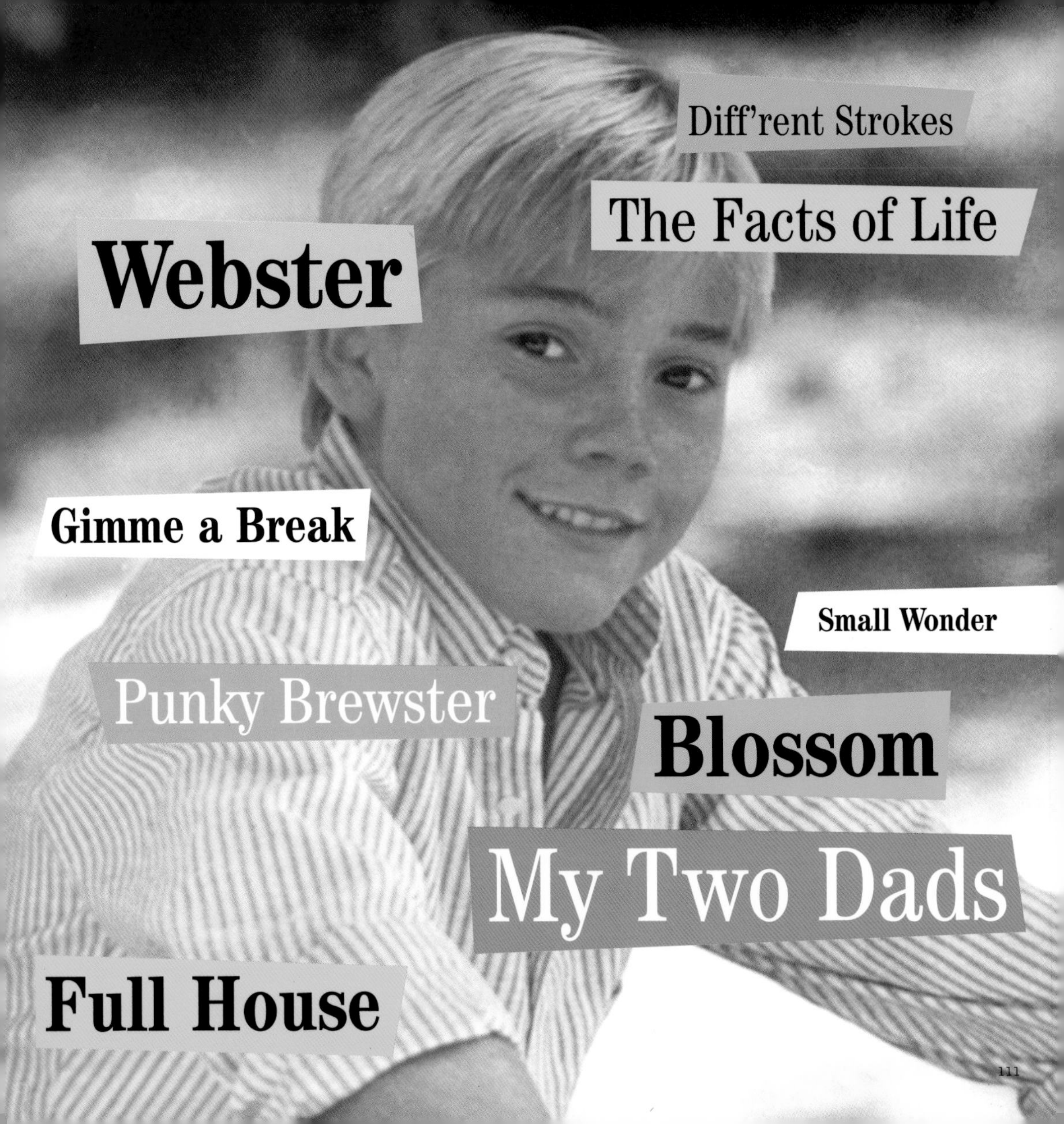

Diff'rent Strokes

The Facts of Life

Webster

Gimme a Break

Small Wonder

Punky Brewster

Blossom

My Two Dads

Full House

111

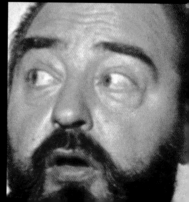

**Manly, yes.
But I like it, too!**

WOULDN'T YOU LIKE
TO BE A PEPPER, TOO?

You're soaking in it!

WHEN YOU'RE OUT OF SCHLITZ, YOU'RE OUT OF BEER!

**Please, don't squeeze
the Charmin!**

Leggo my Eggo!

I CAN BRING HOME THE BACON,
FRY IT UP IN A PAN...

Pass the cookies and pass the cow. Pillsbury cookies and cow, WOW!

Towers. Masterpiece Theatre. Upstairs, Downstairs. Flambards. Absolutely Fabulous. Dr. Who. The Young Ones. Monty Python. Benny Hill. Fawlty

★ THE BRADY BUNCH ★
★ THE PARTRIDGE FAMILY ★
★ ROOM 222 ★
★ THE ODD COUPLE ★

Mr. Microphone

Zamfir, master of the pan flute

ch-ch-ch-**chia!**

GLH

It slices, it dices!

Turn ordinary bottles into attractive glasses!

Ronco

Ginsu Knives

Seal-A-Meal

clap on, clap off!

Popeil's Pocket Fisherman

Thigh Master

I've **fallen** and I can't get up!

Flowbee

John Candy ○ **Bob and Doug McKenzie**
○ **Joe Flaherty** ○ "The Great White North" ○
Eugene Levy ○ Andrea Martin ○ **Rick Moranis**
○ **Edith Prickley** ○ Catherine O'Hara ○
Tex and Edna Boil's Organ Emporium
○ Dave Thomas ○ **Guy Caballero**
○ **"The Sammy Maudlin Show"** ○
"Days of the Week" ○ **"The Cruising**
Gourmet" ○ **"The Fracases,**
America's Nastiest Couple"
○ **Billy Sol Hurok**
& Big Jim McBob
○ Count Floyd ○ "Scaaary!"

Things Go Better with Coke **It's the Real Thing** I'd Like to Buy the World a Coke
Coke Adds Life Coke Is It **Red, White and You** Can't Beat the Feeling

Catch the wave. Coke

Think Young! Come Alive! You're in the Pepsi Generation! Pepsi Pours It On!
You've Got a Lot to Live, Pepsi's Got a Lot to Give Join the Pepsi
People, Feelin' Free! Have a Pepsi Day! Take the Pepsi Challenge!

123

The Newlywed Game

BERT CONVY

DICK CLARK

"*Will the real* _____ Name That Tune

PEGGY CASS

please stand up."

Tattletales

Match Game

Split Second

ALAN LUDDEN

It's Your Bet

FAMILY FEUD

KITTY CARLISLE

The Wizard of Odds

The Dating Game

WINK MARTINDALE

Three on a Match

BOB EUBANKS

Truth or Consequences

Joker's Wild

"I'LL TAKE CHARLEY WEAVER TO BLOCK."

"*Enter and sign in, please.*"

Password

Jeopardy!

CAROL MERRILL

Baffle

GENE RAYBURN

Gambit

BILL CULLEN

Concentration

Dealer's Choice

[A MARK GOODSON–BILL TODMAN PRODUCTION]

PETER MARSHALL

Beat the Clock

THE $100,000 PYRAMID

Call My Bluff

CHARLES NELSON-REILLY

PAUL LYNDE

Winning Streak

High Rollers

BOB BARKER

People Do The Craziest Things

The Gong Show

The $1.98 Beauty Contest

That's Incredible!

Kids Are People, Too

The Art Linkletter Show

Real People

America's Funniest Home Videos

The Guinness Book of World Records

Totally Hidden Video

This Is Your Life

Queen for a Day

Smile YOU'RE ON Candid Camera!

STILL THE ONE
THE NETWORK OF THE NEW
THE BEST IS RIGHT HERE ON CBS
COME AND SEE!
THIS IS THE PLACE TO BE
NBCABCCBS

...PUT A TIC TAC IN YOUR MOUTH AND GET A BANG OUT OF LIFE...MM! MM! GOOD! MM! MM! GOOD! THAT'S WHAT CAMPBELL'S SOUPS AKE, MM! MM! GOOD!...I AM STUCK ON BAND-AID AND BAND-AID'S STUCK ON ME... SOMETIMES YOU FEEL LIKE A NUT, SOMETIMES YOU DON'T...

 **Booker**

The Cosby Show

Melrose Place

The Joey Bishop Show

The Brady Brides

 **Fish**

Burke's Law

Burke's Law

Hill Street Blues

Sanford

The Sanford Arms

 **Enos**

Apple's Way

Eight Is Enough

Family

The Family Holvak

The Fitzpatricks

Little House On The Prairie

Mulligan's Stew

The New Land

Shirley

PLOP PLOP PLOP FIZZ FIZZ

TUMS FOR THE TUMMY

(OH WHAT A RELIEF IT IS!)

I can't believe I ate the whole thing... You ate it Ralph, you ate it...

How do you spell relief?

indiGESTion!

142

Didn't find your fondest memory in *Do You Remember TV*? Fax it to us for Volume Three at (212) 575-0070. Or E-mail us your suggestions. Reach us online at TakeUBack@aol.com or at www.doyouremember.com

SEPTEMBER 13, 1974

Friday

AFTERNOON

6 NEWS

8 FARMER'S DAUGHTER (BW)
Katy finds a diary written by Glen's late wife Ann.

27 MOVIE—Science Fiction (BW)
"Missile to the Moon." (1958) Moon mayhem involving escaped convicts, rock creatures and a giant spider. Richard Travis, Cathy Downs. Lido: K.T. Stevens. (2 hrs.)

38 CAN YOU TOP THIS?—Game
Guests: Ernest Borgnine, Phyllis Diller and Soupy Sales.

56 MOVIE—Drama (BW)
"Night unto Night." (1949) The turbulent romance of an epileptic scientist and a grieving widow who meet on Florida's east coast. Ronald Reagan, Viveca Lindfors, Broderick Crawford. Thalia: Rosemary De Camp. Lisa: Osa Massen. Poole: Art Baker. Josephine: Lillian Yarbo. Tony: Craig Stevens. Superior soap opera based on Philip Wylie's novel. (2 hrs.)

12:55 4 10 NBC NEWS—Edwin Newman

1:00 3 MATCH GAME

4 SOMERSET—Serial

5 6 8 9 ALL MY CHILDREN —Serial

7 TRUTH OR CONSEQUENCES

10 JACKPOT!—Game

12 WHAT'S MY LINE?

38 JACK LaLANNE

1:30 3 7 12 AS THE WORLD TURNS —Serial

4 10 JEOPARDY!—Game

5 6 8 9 LET'S MAKE A DEAL —Game

38 FLYING NUN—Comedy
Sr. Bertrille (Sally Field) has a new admirer: a pelican that thinks she's a bird of a feather. Father Sweeney: Harold Gould. Sr. Jacqueline: Marge Redmond.

2:00 3 7 12 GUIDING LIGHT—Serial

4 10 DAYS OF OUR LIVES—Serial

5 6 8 9 NEWLYWED GAME

38 PORKY PIG AND FRIENDS

2:30 3 7 12 EDGE OF NIGHT—Serial

4 10 DOCTORS—Serial

5 6 8 9 GIRL IN MY LIFE

27 FELIX THE CAT

38 BUGS BUNNY AND FRIENDS

56 TENNESSEE TUXEDO

3:00 2 ELLIOT NORTON REVIEWS

3 7 12 PRICE IS RIGHT—Game

4 10 ANOTHER WORLD—Serial

5 6 8 9 GENERAL HOSPITAL —Serial

27 POPEYE—Cartoon

38 BULLWINKLE

56 UNDERDOG

3:30 2 MAGGIE AND THE BEAUTIFUL MACHINE—Exercise

3 RANGER STATION

4 10 HOW TO SURVIVE A MARRIAGE—Serial

5 6 8 9 ONE LIFE TO LIVE —Serial

7 12 MATCH GAME
Scheduled: Richard Dawson, Brett Somers, Richard Long, Kaye Stevens, Jo Ann Pflug, Charles Nelson Reilly. Host: Gene Rayburn.

27 TIMMY AND LASSIE—Drama (BW)
Lassie picks the winning ticket at a raffle—and the number is held by Ruth (June Lockhart).

38 SUPERMAN—Adventure (BW)
A vengeful crook finds the one element that can destroy Superman —

Monday

(4) (10) DAYS OF OUR LIVES—Serial
(5) (6) (8) (9) NEWLYWED GAME
(38) PORKY PIG AND FRIENDS
2:30 (3) (7) (12) EDGE OF NIGHT—Serial
(4) (10) DOCTORS—Serial
(5) (6) (8) (9) GIRL IN MY LIFE
(27) FELIX THE CAT
(38) BUGS BUNNY AND FRIENDS
(56) TENNESSEE TUXEDO
3:00 (2) ANTIQUES
(3) (7) (12) PRICE IS RIGHT—Game
(4) (10) ANOTHER WORLD—Serial
(5) (6) (8) (9) GENERAL HOSPITAL
—Serial
(27) POPEYE—Cartoon
(38) BULLWINKLE
(56) UNDERDOG
3:30 (2) MAGGIE AND THE BEAUTIFUL
MACHINE—Exercise
(3) RANGER STATION
(4) (10) HOW TO SURVIVE A MAR-
RIAGE—Serial
(5) (6) (8) (9) ONE LIFE TO LIVE
—Serial
(7) (12) MATCH GAME
Scheduled: Richard Dawson, Brett
Somers, Scoey Mitchlll, Elaine Joyce,
Fannie Flagg, Charles Nelson Reilly.
Host: Gene Rayburn.
(27) TIMMY AND LASSIE—Drama (BW)
Lassie mysteriously refuses to help
Paul locate a swarm of ladybugs.
(38) SUPERMAN—Adventure (BW)
Superman helps an ex-convict thwart
a blackmailer. George Reeves. Gray-
son: Hugh Beaumont. Maynard: John
Kellogg. Lois: Noel Neill.
(56) BANANA SPLITS
4:00 (2) (36) (44) (53) SESAME STREET
(3) MIKE DOUGLAS
Loretta Lynn is this week's co-host.

Thursday

author Maya Angelou and psychic
Sybil Leek. (90 min.)
(9) UNCLE GUS
(10) BEWITCHED—Comedy
Think it's hard keeping up with a
baby? Try a baby witch! Samantha:
Elizabeth Montgomery.
(56) BATMAN—Adventure
Conclusion. The Penguin (Burgess
Meredith) tries to put his evil master
plan into operation. Batman: Adam
West. Robin: Burt Ward.
5:00 (2) (36) (53) MISTER ROGERS' NEIGH-
BORHOOD—Children
(3) (6) RAYMOND BURR—Crime
Drama
A massive power failure that hits the
city is obviously intended to cover up
a carefully planned crime. Ironside:
Raymond Burr. Dave Spangler: Jack
Albertson. (60 min.)
(5) FBI—Crime Drama
Two fugitives hide out in a California wine-growing area. Their
next job: robbing a bank during
the annual harvest fiesta. Lisa:
Diane Baker. Wilson: Burt Brincker-
hoff. Troy: Robert Duvall. Erskine:
Efrem Zimbalist Jr. (60 min.)
(10) MOD SQUAD—Crime Drama
Pete's concern for a former girl
friend's problems involves him in
her family's corporate power strug-
gle—and a reunion with his mother
(Anita Louise): Claire: Margot Kid-
der. Doug: Mark Goddard. Pete:
Michael Cole. (60 min.)
(38) F TROOP—Comedy
The general (Cliff Arquette) puts
Wild Eagle in command of F Troop.
O'Rourke: Forrest Tucker. Wild Ea-